Returning Home

Criss Wynters

RETURNING HOME

LITTLE CEDAR AND THE RIVER CANOE

Once, long ago, the Occaneechi people traveled the rivers like threads in an excellent weaving. Their canoes carried them to trade, to visit family, and to share stories with other villages. But the world changed.

The paths closed, and the people were told to forget their ways. Three hundred years later, one girl decided it was time to remember.

Her name was Little Cedar, though most people called her Ava at school. But today, she stood on the riverbank, barefoot, with her heart whole of purpose.

"The water is calling me," she whispered, her eyes fixed on the current. Her grandmother's stories echoed in her mind—stories of how the ancestors carved canoes from great trees and followed the rivers home. "I will bring it back," she said aloud, hands on her hips. "I'll bring the canoe back to our people."

Little Cedar knew the old canoe lay hidden deep in the forest. Her grand-mother's voice echoed in her heart:

"Our canoe sleeps where the water meets the cedar trees. Look for the place where the sun breaks through the shadows."

She walked steadily, listening to the calls of the birds, the rustle of leaves, and the quiet beat of her own footsteps. The forest was not just trees — it was home. It remembered her people's footsteps, just as it now remembered hers.

Her fingers brushed the bark of a tall cedar tree. "Thank you for guiding me," she whispered, just as her grandmother had taught her.

After hours of walking, she saw it—the canoe. It lay cradled in the roots of a great cedar, half-covered in moss and vines.

Its once-smooth surface was rough with age, but the shape was precise — strong and steady, like her people.

Her heart filled with awe. She ran her fingers along the canoe's edge. "You've been waiting for us," she said softly. "But I'm here now. We're going home."

With careful hands, she began to clear the vines, feeling the spirit of the canoe waking up beneath her touch.

Bringing the canoe to the river was not easy. Little Cedar pushed and pulled with all her might, her muscles burning. Her breath came in sharp puffs, but she didn't give up.

Her grandmother's words echoed in her mind:

"The river remembers you. The water will help you if you ask."

She paused, eyes closed, and spoke to the water. "River, I am your granddaughter. Help me bring this canoe home."

When she opened her eyes, she saw it: a small fox staring at her from the brush. It tilted its head, then darted off, its bushy tail flashing like fire. The path it left behind was clearer, and Little Cedar followed it.

The canoe touched the water with a soft splash, and for a moment, Little Cedar felt something shift — as if time had turned around to watch.

The water lapped at her feet, cool and sweet. Her heart swelled with pride.

She climbed into the canoe and placed her paddle into the water, just as her grandmother had taught her.

With slow, steady strokes, she guided the canoe downriver. Her body moved like she had done this all her life.

"I am my ancestors. I am their hands, their voice, their dreams," she whispered.

The night sky unfolded above her, stars blinking into place. Her arms ached, but she kept going, guided by the song of frogs and the distant call of an owl.

Her reflection shimmered on the water. For a moment, it wasn't her reflection at all — it was a young Occaneechi woman in regalia, paddling a canoe with strength and grace.

Little Cedar gasped. The reflection changed back, but she felt it in her bones. She carried them all with her.

When Little Cedar's canoe reached the village, her people were already gathered on the shore. Her grandmother stood in the center, her face full of pride and love.

"She's brought it back!" cried one of the children, pointing to the canoe.

Little Cedar's arms were tired, her body sore, but her heart felt light as a feather. She guided the canoe to shore, and her people surrounded her, touching the canoe as if it were a living thing.

Her grandmother's eyes glowed with tears. "You have brought back more than the canoe, my child. You have brought back our spirit."

That night, Little Cedar sat by the fire, her grandmother's arm draped over her shoulders. The smell of cedar wood and roasting corn filled the air.

"Do you see now?" her grandmother asked. "The canoe is not just wood and water. It is the journey itself."

Little Cedar nodded, her eyes reflecting the flames. "I understand now. I'm part of the journey, and so are you."

Her grandmother smiled. "Yes, and now, every child who sees that canoe will remember. They will know where they come from. And one day, they will guide us all home."

Criss Wynters is an acclaimed author and storyteller from the Piedmont region of North Carolina. Celebrated for her dedication to preserving Indigenous oral traditions, Wynters weaves captivating tales that bridge the past and present, ensuring cultural wisdom is passed on to future generations.

Her storytelling journey began at the age of ten, inspired by the beauty of nature and the vibrant heritage of her community. Through her work, she highlights the profound connections between people, the land, and the stories that shape our identities.

Wynters often explores the outdoors when she's not writing, gathering inspiration from her homeland's rivers, forests, and hills. Her books resonate with readers of all ages, fostering a sense of wonder, respect, and cultural appreciation.